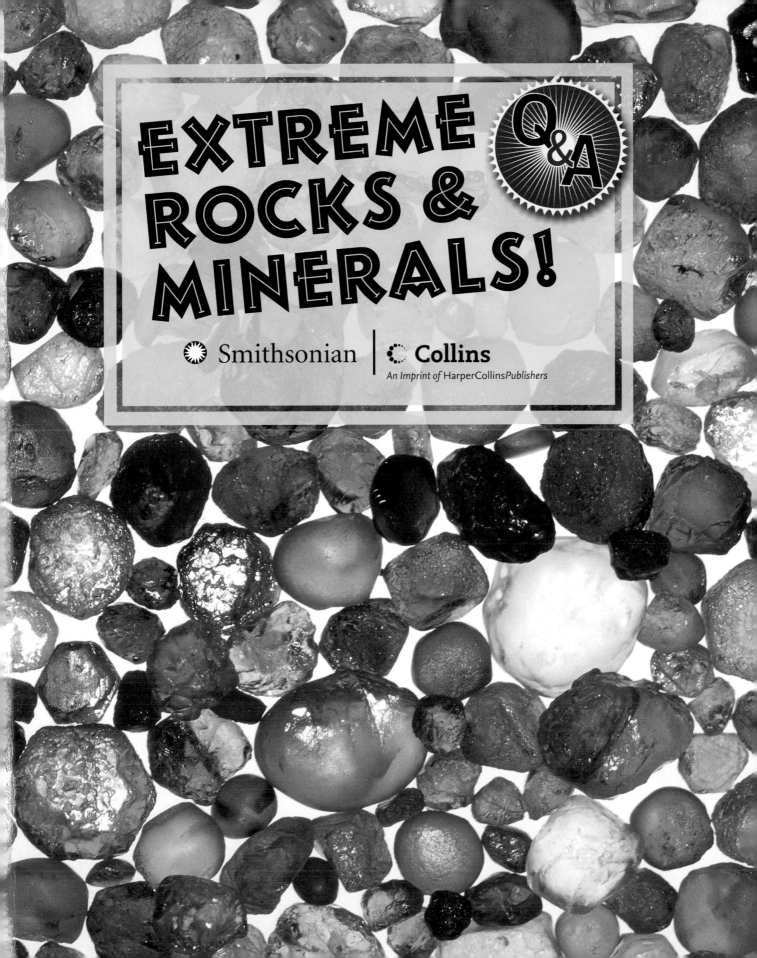

# EXTREME Q&A ROCKS & MINERALS!

**Smithsonian** | **Collins**
*An Imprint of HarperCollinsPublishers*

## Smithsonian Mission Statement

For more than 160 years, the Smithsonian has remained true to its mission, "the increase and diffusion of knowledge." Today the Smithsonian is not only the world's largest provider of museum experiences supported by authoritative scholarship in science, history, and the arts but also an international leader in scientific research and exploration. The Smithsonian offers the world a picture of America, and America a picture of the world.

Special thanks to Jeffrey E. Post, Ph.D., Curator-in-Charge, Mineral Collection, National Museum of Natural History, Smithsonian Institution, for his invaluable contribution to this book.

Special thanks to Professor Marli Bryant Miller, Department of Geological Sciences, University of Oregon, for her invaluable contribution to this book.

This book was created by **jacob packaged goods LLC** (www.jpgglobal.com). **Written by:** Melissa Stewart **Creative:** Ellen Jacob, Jeff Chandler, Kathy Zoehfeld, Andrea Curley

**Photo credits: title page:** © Wayne Scherr/Photo Researchers, Inc.; **page 4:** © Andrew Lambert/Photo Researchers, Inc.; **inset:** Lawrence Lawry/Photo Researchers, Inc.; **page 5, inset:** © Mark A. Schneider/Dembinsky Photo Associates; **page 6:** © E. R. Degginger/Dembinsky Photo Associates; **page 7: top:** © Klaus Guldbrandsen/Photo Researchers, Inc.; **center:** © Mark A. Schneider/Dembinsky Photo Associates; **inset left:** © Lawrence Migdale/Photo Researchers, Inc.; **page 8:** © Terry Whittaker/Photo Researchers, Inc.; **inset left:** © Stephen J. Krasemann/Photo Researchers, Inc.; **inset center:** Chip Clark/Smithsonian Institution; **inset right:** © Mark A. Schneider/Photo Researchers, Inc.; **page 9:** © Robert Pettit/Dembinsky Photo Associates; **page 10, inset:** USGS; **pages 10–11:** Nelson Salting/APImages; **page 12:** © Stephen and Donna O'Meara/Photo Researchers, Inc.; **page 13, top and center:** © Joyce Photographics/Photo Researchers, Inc.; **bottom:** © Doug Martin/Photo Researchers, Inc.; **page 14:** © Martin Bond/Photo Researchers, Inc.; **page 15:** © Richard J. Green/Photo Researchers, Inc.; **pages 16–17:** NASA; **page 18, inset:** © Marli Miller; **page 19:** © George Dineen/Photo Researchers, Inc.; **page 20 inset:** © Art Wolfe/Photo Researchers, Inc.; **pages 20–21:** © Adam Jones/Dembinsky Photo Associates; **page 23, right:** © Roe Intrieri; **left:** © Joyce Photographics/Photo Researchers, Inc.; **page 24:** © Bernhard Edmaier/Photo Researchers, Inc.; **page 25:** © Adam Jones/Dembinsky Photo Associates; **pages 26–27:** © Marilyn Kazmers/Dembinsky Photo Associates; **page 27, inset:** © Jeffrey Grennberg/Photo Researchers, Inc.; **pages 28–29:** Hans Edinger/APImages; **page 30:** © Patti McConville/Dembinsky Photo Associates; **page 31: gneiss:** © Mark A. Schneider/Dembinsky Photo Associates; **marble:** © Marli Miller; **pages 32–33:** © E. R. Degginger/Dembinsky Photo Associates; **pages 34–35:** © Claudia Adams/Dembinsky Photo Associates; **page 35, inset:** © Ben Johnson/Photo Researchers, Inc.; **pages 36–37:** © Adam Jones/Dembinsky Photo Associates; **pages 38–39:** Santiago Llanquin/APImages; **page 39, inset:** © Ben Johnson/Photo Researchers, Inc.; **page 40:** © Mark A. Schneider/Dembinsky Photo Associates; **inset:** courtesy Smithsonian Institution; **page 41:** all courtesy Smithsonian Institution; **pages 42–43:** © Ria Novosti/Photo Researchers, Inc.; **page 43, inset:** © E. R. Degginger/Photo Researchers, Inc.; **page 45:** © Jessica Czajkowski.

# Contents

# WHAT IS A MINERAL?

When you look at a mineral, such as this diamond, you can't see the tiny atoms it is made of. But a model can help you understand a mineral's structure. In this model, the black balls represent the carbon atoms that make up a diamond. The gray pieces represent the bonds between the atoms.

This gold nugget contains billions of gold atoms. When it is refined and combined with other metal, gold can be used to make beautiful jewelry.

**A** **mineral** is a natural, crystalline material that is not alive and has never been alive. Copper and diamonds are minerals, but wood is not. There are currently 4,217 different minerals on Earth.

Like everything in the world, minerals are made of tiny particles called **atoms**. Gold is always made of gold atoms, and diamonds are always made of carbon atoms. Gold and diamonds each contain just one kind of atom, but most minerals contain two or more.

Quartz is one of the most common minerals in Earth's crust. It contains two kinds of atoms—silicon and oxygen. Calcite contains three kinds of atoms—calcium, carbon, and oxygen. Each mineral has its own special arrangement of atoms.

# HOW DO PEOPLE USE MINERALS?

You and your family use minerals every day. Mirrors, computers, and lightbulbs are made of products derived from minerals. So are radios, cell phones, jewelry, and toothpaste. A television set is made of products from at least 35 different minerals.

Gold, silver, diamonds, and rubies can be used to make beautiful jewelry. Fluorite is the main source of the fluoride added to toothpaste and drinking water. It helps keep your teeth strong and healthy. The metals in cars, soda cans, and toasters also come from minerals.

The mineral titanite is used to make a strong metal called titanium, which is used to build airplanes and spacecraft. Halite is processed into the table salt that flavors our food.

**Fluorite crystal**

Titanium rods

Titanium can be extracted from titanite and used in thousands of products—from paper to golf clubs.

Fluoride helps protect your teeth's enamel from plaque and sugars that cause cavities.

**SMITHSONIAN LINK**
Minerals come in a rainbow of colors. Find out why at the National Museum of Natural History.
www.mnh.si.edu/earth/text/2_2_3_1.html

Quartz crystals

Feldspar

Limestone

The white cliffs of Dover, England, are made of limestone.

# WHAT IS A ROCK?

The minerals we use every day come from the earth. Minerals are the basic ingredients of **rocks**. Some rocks contain just one mineral, but most contain two or more. Granite is a rock that usually contains the minerals quartz, feldspar, and mica. Limestone is a rock made of the minerals calcite, dolomite, and aragonite.

Some rocks are smooth and others are rough. Some are flat and others are round. Some rocks are shiny and others are dull. Some rocks have specks or streaks of color. The way a rock looks and feels can help you identify the minerals it is made of.

A rock's appearance and texture can also tell you something about how the rock formed.

When you look at this granite rock, you can easily see the different minerals it contains.

# WHAT IS AN IGNEOUS ROCK?

The word "igneous" means "made from fire." But **igneous rocks** aren't really made from fire. They form when hot, melted rock cools down and hardens.

Deep inside Earth it is very hot—so hot that some of the rock melts and becomes as soft as cooked oatmeal. This melted rock, or **magma**, moves up toward Earth's surface. If it finds or creates an opening in the ground, it spills out as **lava**.

As soon as lava hits air or water, it starts to cool. In a few days or weeks, lava hardens and becomes igneous rock. Over time, piles of igneous rock may build up to form volcanic mountains.

Sometimes magma doesn't rise all the way to Earth's surface. It cools more slowly and forms a different kind of igneous rock.

Pumice is an igneous rock that forms when a volcano spews lava into the air as a frothy mixture of gas bubbles. The holes in pumice make it so lightweight that it can often float in water.

When Mayon Volcano in the Philippines erupted in 2001, sizzling hot lava flowed down its steep slopes. As the lava cooled, it formed igneous rock.

As this lava cools, it is forming a new layer of basalt.

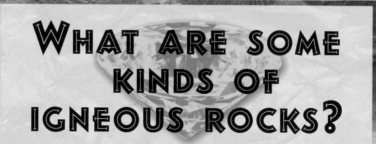

# What are some kinds of igneous rocks?

Basalt and obsidian are igneous rocks that form as lava cools and hardens above-ground. Basalt is usually solid gray or black and very hard. Obsidian is usually brown or black. It has a shiny surface.

Granite and gabbro form as magma cools underground. They contain large **mineral crystals**. Crystals are solid materials, such as minerals, with atoms arranged in repeating patterns. The mineral crystals in granite can be gray, white, pink, or black. Gabbro is mostly gray and white, but it may have some green or black crystals.

# DO ALL IGNEOUS ROCKS CONTAIN MINERAL CRYSTALS?

**W**hen igneous rock forms underground, its minerals cool slowly over thousands of years. There is plenty of time for big, beautiful crystals to form. But when lava erupts out of a volcano, its minerals cool quickly. They don't have time to form large crystals. The crystals in basalt are tiny. Obsidian cools so quickly that it doesn't have crystals.

Because granite (top) cools slowly, it contains large mineral crystals. The crystals in basalt (bottom) are smaller and much harder to see.

Obsidian has a smooth, shiny surface. It is opaque, which means that light cannot pass through it—thus its black color.

**SMITHSONIAN LINK**
Want to learn more about how crystals grow? Take a look at the Smithsonian's "Crystal Growth" web page.
www.mnh.si.edu/earth/text/2_2_2_0.html

Igneous rocks are the most common rocks on Earth's surface.

This photo was taken in Iceland. The black sand beach at the bottom has formed as the incredible basalt columns above it erode, or wear away.

# WHERE ON EARTH ARE IGNEOUS ROCKS?

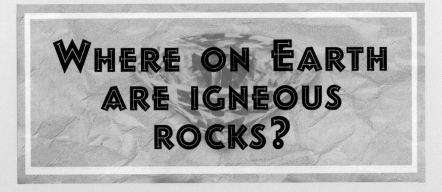

The ocean floor is made of basalt. So are the black sand beaches of Hawaii, Scotland, Greece, Iceland, and New Zealand.

Many volcanic mountains are made of basalt, too. Devil's Tower in Wyoming and the Cascades Range on the western coasts of Canada and the United States contain large amounts of basalt rock. Other mountains, such as Le Puy de Dôme in France and Sugarloaf Mountain in Brazil, are made of granite.

The Andes Mountains in South America contain andesite. Half Dome Mountain in California is made of an igneous rock called granodiorite, and the Glass Buttes in Oregon are made of obsidian.

Half Dome Mountain is one of the most climbed igneous structures in the world. It is located in Yosemite National Park in California.

# WHERE ELSE ARE IGNEOUS ROCKS FOUND?

**A**ll the planets, moons, and other objects in our **solar system** formed about 4.6 billion years ago. They developed from a giant spinning cloud of dust and hot gases.

## Our sun formed at the center of the spinning cloud.

Over millions of years, the rest of the material in the cloud clumped together to form other objects. Eight large objects move around, or orbit, the sun. They are called planets.

The four planets closest to the sun have rocky surfaces. These planets—Mercury, Venus, Earth, and Mars— are made mostly of igneous rock. Many moons, including Earth's moon, are made entirely of igneous rock. So are thousands of smaller objects called **meteoroids**.

The four rocky planets are shown here from left to right: Mercury, Venus, Earth, and Mars.

Igneous rocks are scattered across the surface of Mars. This photo was taken by a robotic machine called the Mars Exploration Rover, which was landed on Mars by a NASA space mission.

**SMITHSONIAN LINK**
Visit the National Museum of Natural History's "The Solar System" exhibition online at
www.mnh.si.edu/earth/text/5_0_0.html

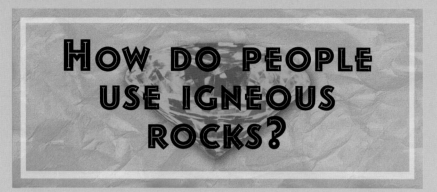

# HOW DO PEOPLE USE IGNEOUS ROCKS?

People use igneous rocks in many ways. Granite and gabbro are strong, beautiful rocks. They are good choices for buildings and statues. The walls of the Empire State Building in New York City are made of white granite and limestone (a sedimentary rock). The Vietnam Veterans Memorial in Washington, DC, is made of polished gabbro.

Gabbro

Gabbro is an igneous rock that forms as magma cools slowly underground.

Giant moai statues made of basalt line the shores of Easter Island in the South Pacific Ocean.

The ancient Egyptians often made statues out of basalt. But the most incredible structures ever made from the hard, black rock are the moai statues on Easter Island. About 400 years ago, native people carved hundreds of giant stone figures and hauled them to the island's shores.

Several groups of native peoples made tools, masks, and jewelry from obsidian. Today, some people rub pumice, a lightweight volcanic rock, on their feet to remove dead skin.

# WHAT IS A SEDIMENTARY ROCK?

The word "sediment" means "to sink down or settle." **Sedimentary rock** is made of sand, mud, pebbles, and tiny pieces of shells that sank to the bottom of lakes and oceans long ago.

The sand, mud, and pebbles were carried to lakes and oceans by winding rivers and whipping winds. The shells drifted down to the bottom when the snails and other sea creatures living in the shells died.

As time passed, layers of sediment slowly built up. The weight of the material on top pressed down on the layers below. Minerals in the water, sand, and pebbles acted like cement. They glued together all the materials to form layers of solid sedimentary rock.

The beautiful layers of rock that we see today in the Grand Canyon are made of sediments, such as sand and mud and the pebbles shown in the inset.

# WHAT ARE SOME KINDS OF SEDIMENTARY ROCKS?

Different kinds of sediments form different kinds of sedimentary rock. Sandstone is made mostly of sandy sediments.

## Mud is the main ingredient of shale and mudstone.

Conglomerate and breccia contain stones and pebbles of all shapes and sizes. The materials in conglomerate have rounded edges, and the materials in breccia have sharp edges.

Limestone and diatomite are made of the shells of tiny ocean creatures. Rock salt is a solid mass of salt left behind when an ancient sea **evaporated**, or changed from liquid water to a gas called water vapor.

# HOW CAN YOU IDENTIFY SEDIMENTARY ROCKS?

If you look carefully at a rock, you can learn a lot about it. If you see layers when you hold a rock at arm's length, it's probably a sedimentary rock. Most sedimentary rocks have small mineral crystals. Some contain tiny bits of pebbles and shells. You might even spot the fossilized bones of an ancient animal in sedimentary rock. Almost all fossils are found in this kind of rock.

This girl is examining a sedimentary rock.

This piece of breccia was collected in Australia. It contains a variety of colorful pebbles.

# WHERE ON EARTH ARE SEDIMENTARY ROCKS?

**M**any of the world's most beautiful natural areas are made of sedimentary rock. The Grand Canyon formed as the Colorado River wore away layer after layer of sedimentary rock. The Painted Desert in Arizona contains many colorful layers of limestone, sandstone, and shale. The Yorkshire Dales in England and the rock falls in Pamukkale, Turkey, are made of sedimentary rock, too.

You can also see beautiful sedimentary features in caves. Most caves form when water slowly eats away at sedimentary rock such as limestone. Inside many caves, water that is full of minerals drips off the ceilings and flows along the floors.

The colorful sedimentary landscape in Arizona's Painted Desert was created about 220 million years ago.

This cavern in Kentucky's Mammoth Cave National Park features many beautiful *stalactites* and *stalagmites*. In some places the stalactites and stalagmites have merged to form thick limestone columns.

Rocky structures shaped like flowers or bubbles or even twisted strands of hair form along cave walls. They are all made of minerals from sedimentary rock.

**SMITHSONIAN LINK**
Want to learn more about how caves form? Go to the Smithsonian's "The Dynamic Earth: Caves" web page.
www.mnh.si.edu/earth/text/3_1_3_1.html

Even though the Egyptians built the Pyramids of Giza thousands of years ago, the giant sandstone structures are still standing.

# HOW DO PEOPLE USE SEDIMENTARY ROCKS?

People have depended on sedimentary rock for thousands of years. Early humans used flint to start fires and to make tools with sharp edges. The ancient Egyptians used sandstone to create the Great Sphinx more than 4,500 years ago.

Both the Egyptians and the Maya used sandstone to build giant pyramids.

The ancient Romans used concrete—a mixture of ground limestone, clay, sand, gravel, and water—to build a great stadium, the Colosseum; a large temple, the Pantheon; and many other buildings.

Today some libraries, schools, and town halls are built with sandstone blocks. Some walls and most building foundations are made of concrete. Chalk, glass, dishes, and the salt you sprinkle on your food are also made from sedimentary rock.

Today some New York City residents live in newer sedimentary structures. Like the Pyramids, these brownstones are made of sandstone.

The word "metamorphic" means "to change in form."

**Forces deep inside Earth have the power to change the minerals inside a rock.**

Eventually a new kind of rock forms.

When igneous rocks or sedimentary rocks get very hot or are squeezed for a long time, they become **metamorphic rock**. Heat and pressure can also change one kind of metamorphic rock into a different kind of metamorphic rock.

Some metamorphic rock is made when hot magma pushes into cracks near Earth's surface. The rock all around the magma gets so hot that the minerals in the rock shift and change.

Metamorphic rock can also form when rocks deep below the surface are pushed, pulled, twisted, and squeezed. These kinds of movements often happen as mountains form.

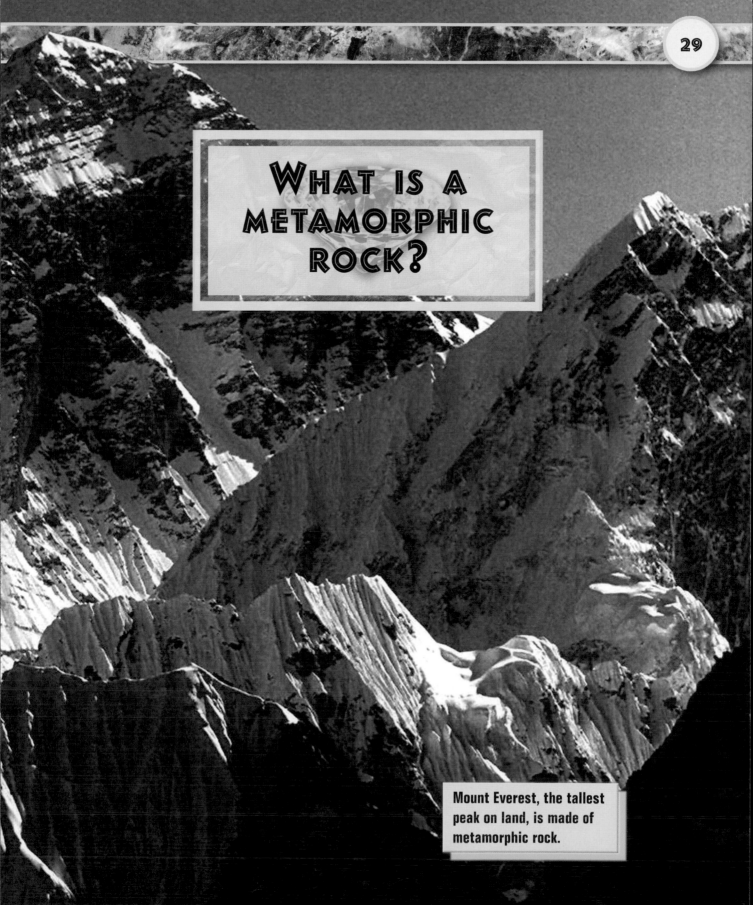

# WHAT IS A METAMORPHIC ROCK?

Mount Everest, the tallest peak on land, is made of metamorphic rock.

# WHAT ARE SOME KINDS OF METAMORPHIC ROCKS?

All metamorphic rocks are hard and durable. But some of them formed from soft sedimentary rocks. When limestone faces heat and pressure, it changes into a beautiful rock called marble. Sandstone becomes quartzite, and shale turns into slate.

The igneous rock basalt changes into a green metamorphic rock called serpentinite. Granite becomes gneiss, one of the hardest rocks in the world.

Metamorphic rocks can undergo changes, too. Slate becomes phyllite, and phyllite turns into schist. Even schist can be changed by heat and pressure. Over time it will become gneiss.

The light and dark bands in gneiss make it easy to identify as a metamorphic rock. Marble (three rocks at right) is used for a variety of purposes, from countertops to Michelangelo's *David*.

# HOW CAN YOU IDENTIFY METAMORPHIC ROCKS?

As heat and pressure form metamorphic rock, the minerals are often sorted to create light and dark bands. The bands are a good way to identify metamorphic rocks. Some metamorphic rocks can be broken into sheets along the edges of the bands. These rocks are perfect for building roofs and walkways.

Because marble is such a beautiful rock, it is a favorite with sculptors. Daniel Chester French's famous marble sculpture of Abraham Lincoln is housed in the Lincoln Memorial in Washington, DC.

**SMITHSONIAN LINK**
Surprised to hear that heat and pressure can change rock? To see the process in action, go to the Smithsonian's "The Dynamic Earth: Rocks Transform" web page.
www.mnh.si.edu/earth/text/3_2_4_0.html

# Where on Earth are metamorphic rocks?

This cut through the Appalachian Mountains shows that they are made of metamorphic rock.

Nearly all of the world's major mountain ranges contain metamorphic rock. The Himalayas, the Alps, the Caledonian Mountains, the Appalachian Mountains, and the Rocky Mountains all contain metamorphic rock.

What caused the heat and pressure that created the metamorphic rock in these mountains? Earth's surface is broken into giant rocky slabs called plates. Even though the ground seems solid and still to us, it is moving very slowly all the time.

**Some of Earth's plates are moving toward one another. Others are moving apart.**

Mountains often form when two plates press together. Over millions of years, the pressure of the bumping plates pushes land together and lifts it up. As the rock is twisted and squeezed, mountains of metamorphic rock rise up to the sky.

The Taj Mahal in Agra, India, houses the tombs of Emperor Shah Jahan and his wife, Mumtaz Mahal. Jahan built the structure after his beautiful young wife died unexpectedly. It took more than 20 years to complete.

# HOW DO PEOPLE USE METAMORPHIC ROCKS?

**M**arble is the most widely used metamorphic rock. It is easy to cut and polish, and comes in white, black, green, red, and yellowish brown. The Washington Monument and the Lincoln Memorial in Washington, DC, are both made of marble. So is the Taj Mahal in Agra, India. People also use marble to make furniture, staircases, floor tiles, and kitchen countertops.

Both marble and serpentinite are carved into statues and made into jewelry. In some places roads are paved with quartzite. Slate is sometimes used to make roof tiles. Graphite and talc are minerals found only in metamorphic rock. The part of a pencil you write with is made of graphite. Talc is a key ingredient in baby powder, paper, paint, soap, and some pottery.

Talc is often added to paints used on boats. It decreases rusting and makes the paint more durable.

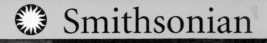
# HOW ARE ROCKS RECYCLED?

**R**ocks are always changing. As magma cools to create new igneous rock, other kinds of rocks are being destroyed. Rock is hard and strong, but wind and water can be even tougher. Crashing ocean waves, fast-flowing rivers, repeated freezing and thawing, and whipping winds slowly wear away, or **erode**, even the hardest rock.

As rocks break down, rivers and streams pick up the sediments and carry them to oceans and lakes. Over time, layers of sediments build up and form sedimentary rock.

Crashing ocean waves are powerful enough to break down all kinds of rock. As the broken pieces build up over time, they may form sedimentary rock.

As Earth's plates move, some sedimentary rock is lifted up and becomes part of the land. If the layers are heated or squeezed, the sedimentary rock may become metamorphic rock. Or if one plate slides below another plate, the rock will melt and become hot, soft magma. Eventually some of the magma will cool to form still more igneous rock.

**SMITHSONIAN LINK**
Get more information about how water recycles rock, with the Mississippi River as the example.
www.mnh.si.edu/earth/main_frames.html

# WHAT IS AN ORE?

**A**n **ore** is any rock or mineral that contains enough metal to be mined for a profit. After an ore is dug out of the ground, it is usually crushed into a powder. Then precious metals can be separated from the powder. Some important metals include iron, copper, aluminum, lead, titanium, and zinc.

To remove iron metal from hematite or magnetite ore, the powder is heated with charcoal and limestone until the iron melts. Copper metal is separated from azurite or malachite ore with chemicals. To remove aluminum metal from bauxite ore, the powder is zapped with electricity. Then people can use the metals to make many of the products you use every day.

> **This metal worker is refining copper from El Teniente, the largest underground copper mine in the world. The mine, which is located in Chile, produces 435,000 tons of copper each year.**

The iron we use to make steel comes from chunks of ore, such as this hematite.

# WHAT IS A GEMSTONE?

A gemstone, or gem, is a large, hard, beautiful mineral crystal that has been cut and polished. Fluorite, calcite, and rhodochrosite are all eye-catching mineral crystals, but they aren't usually made into gemstones. They are soft and scratch easily, so they aren't the best choices for jewelry.

Topaz, garnet, and turquoise are all beautiful and durable gemstones. They are called semiprecious because they are fairly common and therefore not too expensive.

Sapphires, rubies, and emeralds are all precious gemstones. They cost a lot of money because they are rare. Diamonds can cost even more.

Diamond is the hardest known mineral, and it sparkles beautifully.

Emerald is a green variety of the mineral beryl. This crystal was mined in Colombia.

The Hooker Emerald

(left to right) Rosser Reeves Ruby, Shepard Yellow Diamond, Portuguese Diamond, Blue Heart Diamond

The Hope Diamond

Oppenheimer Diamond crystal

The Carmen Lúcia Ruby (left) and fire opals (below)

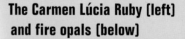

After they have been cut and polished, mineral crystals become sparkling gems.

**SMITHSONIAN LINK**
Learn more about some of the world's most amazing diamonds at the Smithsonian's "The Splendor of Diamonds" web page.
www.mnh.si.edu/exhibits/si-gems

# WHERE ON EARTH ARE GEMSTONES?

Some of the biggest and most valuable gemstones are found in igneous rocks that formed slowly underground. The rocks and their load of mineral crystals come to the surface as mountains form. As time passes, wind and water wear away the rock around the mineral crystals.

Most diamonds form in a kind of igneous rock called kimberlite. The rock is named after the town of Kimberley, South Africa. The major diamond producers are Australia, South Africa, Botswana, Congo, Canada, and Russia.

Brazil is a rich source of gems, including topaz, aquamarine, tourmaline, and some emeralds.

Sri Lanka is a tiny island country off the coast of India. Some people call it Gem Island because many rubies, sapphires, garnets, and other gems have been found there.

Workers search for diamonds at a mine in the Republic of Sakha, an independent state in the Russian Federation. Ninety-nine percent of all Russian diamonds come from Sakha.

**SMITHSONIAN LINK**
Want to learn even more about rocks and minerals? You can get started at the Smithsonian's "Three Rocks and Their Minerals" web page.
www.mnh.si.edu/earth/text/3_1_2_1.html

This diamond crystal is embedded in kimberlite rock found in Kimberley, South Africa.

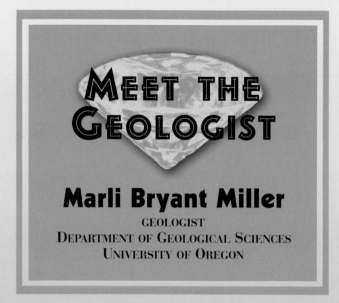

# MEET THE GEOLOGIST

## Marli Bryant Miller

GEOLOGIST
DEPARTMENT OF GEOLOGICAL SCIENCES
UNIVERSITY OF OREGON

## When you were growing up, did you want to be a scientist? Or something else?

My favorite classes were English and history. They taught me to think critically and write. I found science and math to be pretty abstract until I took geology in college. Geology somehow made all the science concepts more meaningful for me.

## What do you do most days? Where and when do you do your research?

My days are split between teaching and research. For teaching, I spend a lot of time preparing handouts and slide presentations, running field trips, and grading papers. I do most of my fieldwork in Death Valley, California. It's too hot to work there in the summer, so I usually go in the winter.

## What do you like most about your job? What do you like least about your job?

I like traveling to amazing places to study geology or teach it to others. I have traveled to Colorado, British Columbia, and the Republic of Kyrgyzstan in Central Asia to do field-work. I like to lead my classes on field trips too. At the University of Oregon, I've been able to take groups of students to places throughout Oregon, and even Death Valley and Montana!

I don't like that I'm always too busy to calm down and be still. But at least I'm busy with stuff that I like!

## What is the most important question you are trying to answer with your research?

I'm trying to understand how fault zones allow areas to rise up high above the earth—and Death Valley is a wonderful place for that. There, the mountains rise directly above the valley floor along fault zones—and because it is so dry, it's easy to see the features that give clues to the faults' histories.

## If you couldn't be a scientist, what would you want to be?

If I weren't a scientist, I'd like to be a photographer. I'd spend a lot of time outside, focusing on the landscapes I have come to love through geology.

## What was the most exciting thing that happened to you in your job?

About six years ago, I was in Kyrgyzstan with my student Craig. We realized that many of the fault zones causing today's mountains to rise were active hundreds of millions of years ago during another mountain-building event.

## Do you work by yourself or with other people?

I do a lot of fieldwork by myself, but I exchange ideas with other people all the time. And we like to simply hang out and share one another's company.

## If I want to be a scientist when I grow up, what should I study now?

Study the subjects you like the most—as you learn more and more about them, you'll naturally branch into other things. Don't make the mistake I made: not going to the teacher for help when I got confused. Get all the help you can! Most teachers like it when you come for extra help because they see you're interested.

# GLOSSARY

**atom**—The smallest unit of an object, material, or living thing. Everything on Earth is made of atoms.

**erode**—To slowly wear away rock or other materials by the action of wind, water, or ice.

**evaporate**—To change from liquid to a gas called vapor.

**igneous rock**—A kind of rock that forms when magma cools and hardens.

**lava**—Magma that spills out onto Earth's surface.

**magma**—Hot, melted, or partially melted rock found below Earth's surface.

**metamorphic rock**—A kind of rock that forms when heat and pressure change the minerals in igneous rock or sedimentary rock.

**meteoroid**—A chunk of rock in space. When a meteoroid hits Earth or another object in space, it is called a meteorite.

**mineral**—A natural solid inorganic material with a specific chemical makeup and structure.

**mineral crystal**—A natural solid material made of atoms or molecules (groups of atoms) arranged in a repeating pattern.

**ore**—A rock or mineral that contains enough metal to be mined for a profit.

**rock**—A natural solid material made of one or more minerals.

**sedimentary rock**—A kind of rock that forms as layers of sand, mud, pebbles, and pieces of shells build up and are pressed and cemented together.

**solar system**—All the objects that orbit the sun or are influenced by it.

**stalactite**—A buildup of calcite (including limestone, chalk, and marble) from the roof of a cave that forms in the shape of an icicle.

**stalagmite**—A buildup of calcite (including limestone, chalk, and marble) from the floor of a cave that forms in the shape of an icicle.

Diamonds

# MORE TO SEE AND READ

## WEBSITES

There are links to many wonderful web pages in this book. But the web is constantly growing and changing, so we cannot guarantee that the sites we recommend will be available. If the site you want is no longer there, you can always find your way to plenty of information about rocks and minerals and a great learning experience through the main Smithsonian website: www.si.edu.

Learn more about rocks and minerals at: www.fi.edu/tfi/units/rocks/rocks.html

For great images and information, visit Harvard University's Mineralogical Museum online at: www.fas.harvard.edu/%7egeomus/collections.htm

Find out how to safely collect rocks and minerals at: www.sciencemaster.com/jump/earth/rock_collecting.php

For help identifying rocks and minerals, try this website: www.minerals.net/gemstone/index.htm

Want to know more about diamonds? Check out this web page on the American Museum of Natural History's website: www.amnh.org/exhibitions/diamonds/indicator.html

## SUGGESTED READING

*National Audubon Society First Field Guide: Rocks and Minerals* by Edward Ricciuti and Margaret W. Carruthers. Use this great guide to identify the rocks you find in your yard, in a local park, or on a hike in a natural area.

*If You Find a Rock* by Peggy Christian, photographs by Barbara Hirsch Lember. This beautifully written book shares the wonders of rocks with young readers.

*Let's Go Rock Collecting* by Roma Gans, illustrated by Holly Keller. This book is a fun look at how rocks form and how people have used rocks throughout history. Some basic information about rock collecting is included.

*The Pebble in My Pocket* by Meredith Hooper, illustrated by Chris Coady. This award-winning story traces one pebble's history as the face of Earth changes.

*Rock and Gem* by R. L. Bonewitz. Chockful of great information and stunning photographs, this book is a must read.

*Rocks and Minerals* by Edward Ricciuti. A simple introduction to the three kinds of rocks, the rock cycle, and more.

*The National Gem Collection* by Jeffrey Post. A beautiful summary of the Smithsonian gem collection.

# INDEX